Grandma's Guide To Gluten Free Cooking

GLUTEN FREE, WHEAT FREE, DAIRY FREE, EGG FREE, PEANUT FREE

Barbara Wells

Bloomington, IN  Milton Keynes, UK

authorHOUSE®

AuthorHouse™
1663 Liberty Drive, Suite 200
Bloomington, IN 47403
www.authorhouse.com
Phone: 1-800-839-8640

AuthorHouse™ UK Ltd.
500 Avebury Boulevard
Central Milton Keynes, MK9 2BE
www.authorhouse.co.uk
Phone: 08001974150

As I wrote this book, I ensured all products and ingredients were free of wheat, gluten, dairy, peanuts and eggs. However, manufacturers often change their ingredients without notice. Therefore, we recommend always reading labels for yourself before consuming any product.

First published by AuthorHouse   1/30/2007

ISBN: 978-1-4259-8701-5 (sc)
ISBN: 978-1-4259-8700-8 (hc)

Printed in the United States of America
Bloomington, Indiana

This book is printed on acid-free paper.

Dedication

This book is dedicated to my grandchildren, Brandon and Maria. Without their special dietary needs this book would have never happened.

I have often joked that I don't know what I want to do when I grow up. I cannot imagine anything more rewarding than to have given of myself to these precious children.

Also, my thanks go to my husband, Bob, and to my son and daughter in law, Brian and Mindy. They never fail to encourage my efforts and to applaud my results. I so appreciate their loving support.

Contents

Grandma's Inspiration

My story begins about 4 years ago when my grandson, Brandon, was restricted to a diet free of gluten, wheat, eggs, dairy, and peanuts.

I was totally bewildered. How could I possibly cook properly for him and his family? I only remember once that I wept in my kitchen pantry out of frustration, but many times I felt that inadequate.

Brandon's mom gave me a couple of recipes, which I prepared on every visit. I also had a house rule that no one was allowed to eat forbidden foods in his presence. I felt that I was doing all that I could until one innocent remark changed my life.

We were in a grocery store and Brandon took my hand, led me to a display, and said longingly, "Look, Nana, those are called muffins". It brought tears to my eyes, and I vowed to myself that I would learn to cook delicious foods - gluten, wheat, dairy, egg, and peanut free.

It has been a journey of trial and error. I cannot tell you that I have successes every time, but imagination and persistence has paid off. I have felt led to write this book, and it is my wish that it will help your family as much as it has helped mine.

Barbara Wells

Emphasis of Book

This book has been developed with an emphasis on baked goods. In my opinion, that is the most difficult area for gluten, wheat, dairy, and egg free.

There are many more mixes on the market now, but often the results tend to be dry and crumbly. I experiment to make the batters moist and of the right consistency. Also, it is crucial that you not over bake.

I have taken many of my old recipes and adapted then to fit this diet. Hopefully you will be inspired to do the same.

Quite often I will bake the sweet breads and cakes in muffin tins. Cupcakes or muffins are easy to store in the freezer and you can thaw them as needed. When your child needs a treat for a school lunch, school party or birthday party, just ice a cupcake and put in a small container. Never again will they be deprived while the other children have treats.

Our Story

Let food be thy medicine and
medicine be thy food~ Hippocrates

If you ask any parent what their greatest fear is I would presume that without a doubt a 100% would answer, "*Losing my child*". Second only to "*the death of my child*" losing a child is one of every parent's greatest gut-wrenching fears. They might lose them in a crowded mall, at the park, or at the local grocery store. When you are drawn into listening to the terrible tale of a parent pleading for the return of their lost child you often hear them say, "*but they were **right** there...right under my nose...and **I lost them**"*.

Any parent or loved one of a child that has either entered the world of ASD or *brushed* the world of ASD, you ***know*** the feeling of losing your child. They may be physically with you but parts of them are *lost*. Sometimes they're unable to reach into your world at all and sometimes with the feeling that you can see them, you can *almost* reach them but can't quite grasp their hand and pull them back to you. Or, what if you have a child that is chronically ill? And, after multiple trips to your pediatrician, multiple pharmaceutical medications, or perhaps other interventions such as Speech, Occupational Therapy, Sensory Integration therapy, etc., they continue to be sick or get sicker?

"The doctor of the future will no longer treat the human frame with drugs, but rather will cure and prevent disease with nutrition." Thomas Edison

Our beautiful son was born right after Thanksgiving in 1999. He was 3 weeks early and born on my mother-in-law's birthday. My husband jokes that it was the ultimate "suck up". Having just turned 31, I was a new mother and overjoyed to begin my journey into motherhood. I distinctly remember the exact moment when the pediatrician did her initial examination on Brandon just hours after his birth. With the stethoscope encircling her neck she looked up and smiled and said, "He's perfect". She was right.

Brandon slept a lot, like most newborns. He rarely cried, and he was a happy baby. He was taken to every well child visit on time and every instruction from our new pediatrician was followed to a T, including **all** vaccinations. And later, when he became physically ill, all medications were adhered to exactly as prescribed. I remember asking the pediatrician if ALL of the vaccinations and repeated doses of medications were absolutely necessary. She assured me they were not only necessary but also that I was being careless if I did not follow the full vaccine schedule exactly as outlined. I was not given a list of risks factors; I was not educated about themerosal, or the option to get single doses of the vaccines. I didn't know. I blindly followed *their* advice. I almost lost my child because of it and the thief was right there, right under my nose.

"The human body heals itself and nutrition provides the resources to accomplish the task." Roger Williams Ph.D. (1971)

Our first clue that something was *not right* was about the time Brandon turned 15 months old. I describe it as his nose started running and didn't stop for another 2 years. As unbelievable as that sounds, it is not far from the truth. During those 2 years I repeatedly took him to multiple doctor appointments. There was Pediatrician 1, 2, and 3, an Allergist (the best guy in town), and an

ENT. All were happy to give me prescription medications to stop the runny nose, ear infections, sinus infections, croup that continuously cycled through his little body. But, the thing was no matter how much medication I gave him (at one time it was 6 prescriptions not including the constant cycle of antibiotics) he continued to be sick, getting sicker and hitting a plateau with his development. The ENT performed surgery to remove his adenoids and put tubes in both ears. She *promised* me "this will do the trick". It didn't. He had an ear infection so bad it lasted for about 7 weeks. When I insisted on a "culture" to find out why none of their high-powered antibiotics could cure it, I soon found my answer. It was yeast, oozing right out of his ear.

At this time my mother, a retired speech pathologist, had told me about a conference she had attended that described how yeast could become overgrown in children's bodies and cause health, behavior, or developmental problems. It sounded unlikely to me, but out of desperation to find *something, anything,* that would help my son I took the information to my team of specialists. They all treated me like I was crazy to mention such a correlation. I sat on it a while, but investigated on the Great Plains Laboratory website that gave detailed description of what yeast could do to a body. It made sense to me that with the numerous courses of antibiotics that my son had been prescribed that the *good* bacteria in his gut was probably wiped out by this yeast. And this yeast might be what was contributing to his illness. I wanted a test. Not one of my team of specialists would order it for me. So, as my first act of defying mainstream medicine, I asked the Great Plains Lab for a referral of a doctor that would perform the yeast test (organic acids). That referral saved my son from the horrible world of ASD.

Meanwhile, right before Brandon's adenoids were yanked out, my Parent Educator from Parents As Teachers said, "You might want to get a speech evaluation". "Why?" I thought, "Every test you've ever done on him has been fine". I took him for that initial evaluation and was told, "He's fine, he's a boy, and he's had lots of ear infections. Come back in 6 months but he's fine, don't worry". I immediately thought, "So why do I have to come back in 6 months if he's fine?"

During that 6-month waiting period, he was prescribed even more antibiotics, giving him a total of 9 courses of antibiotics in just 11 months. And all of his symptoms worsened. Ear infections, sinus infections, croup, severe skin eczema and rash but something more subtle was happening. The eye contact started to wane, and I would go downstairs to his play room and cars would be lined up perfectly end to end. He would repeat instead of answer me. "Do you want to go outside?" He would respond "outside?" Something was happening to him, it was subtle but I was *losing* him, right under my nose.

> *"God, in His infinite wisdom, neglected nothing and if we would eat our food without trying to improve, change or refine it, thereby destroying its life-giving elements, it would meet all requirements of the body." Jethro Kloss*

The Internet led me to sites on autism. Autism? What is autism anyway? Didn't several professional football players have a child with autism? Wasn't Rainman autistic? My son is not autistic, was he? The thing about ASD is every case is different; no two children are exactly alike and can in fact be very different. I looked at the checklist and checked it over and over. He had some of the things on the list but not enough to put him "on the spectrum" but enough that "you might want to get an evaluation". What? Autism? Where did this come from? Didn't that first pediatrician say "he's perfect, with her huge smile"? Didn't she? From that moment I **had** to have THE evaluation. I had to know. Whatever *it* was I *had* to know. So the official journey began...away from "mainstream" medicine. Away from physicians who treat with pharmaceutical medications first instead of finding root causes or triggers to the illness and treating the whole body with nutrition, supplements, and other holistic treatments.

Little did I know that the answer was not in the evaluation, in fact, by the time we had THE evaluation my son didn't fit the criteria for any official diagnosis or label. But he was still physically ill and still had speech and fine motor deficits.

> "The consideration of man's body has not changed to meet the new conditions of this artificial environment that has replaced his natural one. The result is that of perceptual discord between man and his environment. The effect of this discord is a general deterioration of man's body, the symptoms of which are termed disease." Professor Hilton Hotema

I won't take you down our long and arduous journey step by step. What I will tell you is that due to a genetic predisposition that is relatively common, due to being exposed to over 80 times the allowable limit of mercury at 2, 4, and 6 months of age from the required vaccines per the AAPA recommendations, due to being given way too many courses of antibiotics and developing a "leaky gut" that caused multiple food allergies and many other factors, we almost lost our son to neurodevelopmental deficits that could have been preventable. Our son's neurodevelopmental deficits *could have* been diagnosed as something on the ASD spectrum. Fortunately, we were spared that experience. If we had received such a diagnosis, we would have been patted on the head and told "sorry, no cure". That is so far from the truth. After seeking the advice of numerous physicians throughout the Midwest, we finally found someone that could truly help us start to complete the pieces of our medical puzzle. It isn't and wasn't one thing, one cause, one cure, one treatment. Thousands of dollars and a lot of self education later, one of the treatments that we offer our son to assist his body to become well again and move towards optimal health is a diet free of gluten, casein, peanuts, and eggs. Many people have food allergies and sensitivities that can be helped with a certain *food allergy* diet. In fact, my daughter whose only symptom was eczema that showed up around 3 years of age was also "cured" with a diet free of gluten, dairy, peanuts, and eggs.

This is only one piece of our puzzle, and it was overwhelming when we first started our special diet. Prior to food allergies, I used to have a problem deciding what to fix my family for dinner. When we first started our new diet, it became even more of an albatross. Every 4-6 hours when a mealtime rolled around, I felt like I was living a bad dream and taking a test for a class I did not ask to be enrolled in. Little by little, I learned and improved as a cook to a whole new world of cooking. Along, with Speech Therapy, Occupational Therapy, and vitamin supplements, I was encouraged by the improvement and elimination of all previous symptoms that Brandon had experienced. I wouldn't have believed it had I not experienced it.

At 3 years of age, our son was 10 months speech delayed, was very ill, and had fine motor deficits. He had an IEP, attended multiple sessions of Speech Therapy, Occupational Therapy, and Language, Social and Fine Motor groups. At age 5 he entered kindergarten, lost his IEP and his need for additional therapies and had a marvelous kindergarten year. His first grade year has started off amazingly well. He is excelling at his academic milestones, plays a variety of sports, has a lot of great friends and is a very happy kid. I fix his lunch daily and bring all of his snacks to school, parties and play dates. But, what a small price to pay for a child that is WELL! I often wonder how many other children and their parents are handed a label (the medical community prefers the term diagnosis) and are given no hope of improvement, healing or recovery. You name it ADD/ADHD, Autism, Asperger's, Learning Disabled etc. Or maybe it is just severe allergies, eczema, asthma, or other "hard to diagnose" maladies. This is a tragedy because the right help at the right time, consistently over time can change a child's life, not to mention their parent's lives. Diet can be a part of your child's puzzle, and there are tools to figure it out and get the right help you need at the right time.

> *"I am now convinced that most chronic medical conditions can be helped significantly by a healthy diet. Sinus Survival Robert S. Ivker, M.D. Member of the American Holistic Medical Association*

I didn't realize until we were forced into this lifestyle that so much of everything we do in our culture is surrounded by and immersed in food. We create reasons to celebrate with food. Sunday school-snack. School-two snacks. Birthday parties for the party *and* at school. We give and receive food rewards for learning to read, learning to count, learning to spell. We give and receive food rewards for good behavior; after schools pick me up, and during all play dates. I haven't even touched on the Holidays yet. Ahhh, food, and you feel like you or your loved ones are the only ones in the entire world not allowed to eat pizza, ice cream, cookies, etc. The "regular" grocery store becomes your enemy, and you dread meal times. You feel this way at first until you magically watch you or your loved one's health improve dramatically. Then it becomes clear that you are absolutely doing the right thing. Although, to many people, you are living against the grain (no pun intended). It is still difficult, but you know you can and will prevail over this seemingly overwhelming obstacle. You will wonder, "How can certain foods that everyone else commonly eats make me or my loved one sick? I never knew, why didn't my doctor tell me, and why isn't this more widely known?"

My reaction to this question was one of anger...."WHY DIDN'T MY TEAM OF SPECIALISTS KNOW ABOUT THIS AND WHY DIDN'T THEY HELP OUR FAMILY?" If you're angry, work to release it. It will not serve you; only harm you and your loved ones. The simple truth is most Medical Doctors (MD's) aren't taught about nutrition in Medical School. Ok, to be fair perhaps they might have had **one** class. But, most MD's aren't taught to "heal" or search for answers related to food, environment, or taught a holistic approach to healing. Most MD's are taught a certain way of treating which looks at a certain protocol that treats a person with symptoms as "sick". As a result they are usually then treated with a protocol of Pharmaceutical Medications. We were even told my son didn't have *any* food allergies. None! How can there be such a difference of opinion from one doctor to another? By the grace of God and blind Faith, we dove into our first new doctor's (Dr. Jeremy Baptist) protocol of an allergy elimination diet and nutritional supplements. It was hard; I cried my way through Whole Foods Market. I thought, "We can never live this way". But, two months after starting this new diet, all physical symptoms, including ear infection, sinus infection, and croup etc. were gone, and have never returned. All Pharmaceutical Medications were gone. Had I not lived through this I would have never believed it. With persistence and the help of Dr. John Hicks and Pathways Medical Advocates, we were given a protocol of diet and nutritional supplements and other holistic medical modalities that helped my son's body heal. The chronic infections were finally gone. And with the help of some very knowledgeable Speech and Occupational therapists, by Kindergarten, my son needed no additional support services. He became a thriving full-day Kindergartener, soccer and basketball player, and most importantly a healthy, happy boy!

> *"Small things with great love... It's not how much we do, but how much love we put into the doing. And it is not how much we give, but how much we put into the giving. To God there is nothing small..."* **Mother Theresa**

We now know these multiple food allergies are the result of an immune system shift caused by predisposing genetic factors and environmental triggers. A leaky gut caused by repeated and prolonged antibiotic use precluded the food allergies. Remember, when my daughter started to have eczema, I sought out the same treatment. When she follows a GF/CF diet, her skin is eczema free. I learned that sometimes food allergies could present one set of symptoms for one person and a whole other set of symptoms for another. Food allergies or sensitivities can cause multiple "disease-like" or "behavioral" symptoms that are commonly treated with Pharmaceutical Medications.

When I started our new way of cooking and eating four years ago, I limped along, dreading meal after meal. I would get a new cookbook, get energized and then look at the list of ingredients. Not only did I have no idea what some of the ingredients were, I had no idea where to find them. I felt as if someone had dropped me in a foreign land without a map. I improved over time with seeking and finding new recipes, sources, and just plain awareness. But, I still grieved for a world free of special diets and foods, reading every label, and being worried sick when a mistaken infraction occurred.

Thank goodness for my mother in law who has always been a gifted cook. She is known for taking a recipe and tinkering with it until she brings it "to the next level". She adds or removes certain spices and other ingredients until it is better than good! Anyone who has had the pleasure of setting down to dine with her has been given a treat. Therefore, it was only natural that she decided to put her gifts in the kitchen to good use. She started tweaking old family favorite recipes so that both of my children could enjoy them just like the rest of the family. She started experimenting with muffins and it went on from there. Cookies, cakes, and treats of all kinds. The next thing you know we have an entire Thanksgiving, Christmas, and Easter dinners that are GF/CF, peanut and egg free. And, they are delicious! So we began to say, "Barbara, you need to write a cookbook. Do you know how many people would benefit from your ideas, recipes, and knowledge?"

And, so she did. You get to experience the benefits of what the love of a very dedicated Nana can do for her grandchildren. May you enjoy the recipes in this cookbook as much as our family does...may it make your life in the kitchen just a little bit easier and ease the burden of bringing great food to your family. Whatever the reason you have to follow a "special" diet, just know that nothing is as important as your health! I hope this book helps you achieve optimum Health like it has brought to my family. It is such a treat to be able to go visit her and my father in law and not have to pack *all* of my children's food. It is such a gift to know my husband and I can take a vacation and I knew she could handle the diet. Many people I know don't have such a wonderful support system. I hope you do.

For whatever reason that you are using this cookbook, I know you will enjoy these recipes just as much as we currently do. I wish this book had been available when I started this journey 4 years ago. Use it and enjoy...don't be afraid to experiment and put your own twists on things. These recipes opened up a whole new world to me, and I am so grateful. This book was born out of love. She wanted her grandchildren to have and experience the "goodness" of food with great flavor and texture that "the rest of the world" commonly does. They now do. No more dreading meals, especially Holidays...Barbara's got you covered in this fantastic book.

I know this road is less traveled and difficult at times, but you can never put a price or your health. There are too many good food options to not pursue this type of treatment. Trust me you'll be glad you did.

Keep in mind that making sudden drastic changes to your diet can be a recipe for failure. However, when forced with using your diet as a means to optimal health, sometimes it is necessary to make drastic changes. This book is a great place to start and build upon the knowledge you will acquire. This cookbook is so great because it uses simple techniques that anyone cook can handle.

Thank you, Barbara for many things. My children are so lucky to have a Nana who loves them so much. I feel inspired to think that so many others will benefit from your efforts and enjoy the fruits of your labor.

Throughout this journey that we have been on I have to say that there is no doubt in my mind that God led me to find and pursue resources that completed the pieces of our puzzle and bring healing to our family. I would like to pause to give all of my heartfelt gratitude to Him. If you need additional help beyond the scope of this book, I am available per in home or phone consultation to help you unravel the world of special diets. Please visit my website at www.wellcosystems.com. And, stay tuned for future volumes...Barbara keeps tweaking and creating, and there are many more recipes to enjoy!

Mindy Wells

Helpful Hints

- Regular brands of flavorings (vanilla, butter, etc.) contain alcohol which is often wheat based. Frontier and Simply Organic are two brands that are alcohol and gluten free.

- Always read the ingredients listed on products. Companies do make changes from time to time. Call them if in doubt.

- Gluten Free baked goods are often dry and crumbly. Try to moisten your batters. Applesauce helps in some recipes.

- Do not over bake gluten free baked goods.

- All of the muffin and cupcake recipes from this book freeze well. Place in air tight containers.

- When warming up baked goods in the microwave, do not over heat. Start with 20-30 seconds at first.

- Fleischman's Unsalted Margarine is dairy free.

- Always spray muffin pans, cookie sheets, and cake pans with a spray oil. I use Spectrum high heat canola spray oil.

- Pam no stick cooking spray has grain alcohol which is wheat based.

- Do not spray your baking pan when baking angel food cake.

- Modified food starch can be a problem. When you see that term listed on a product's ingredient list, call the company.

- Use aluminum free baking powder. There are several different brands available. These are readily available at health food stores and some grocery stores.

- When bananas over ripen, just put them in the freezer. You can thaw them at room temperature or in your microwave at 50% power until softened.

- There are several nut butters on the market, including almond, cashew, and macadamia. One of the best is Nonuts Golden Pea Butter.

- Dry jello (regular or sugar free) can be used to flavor baked goods.

- Cinnamon sugar sprinkled in the bottom of cake or muffin pans and on top of batters adds good flavor and color.

- For baking, I dilute Vance's Potato Milk - 1 rounded c. powdered milk to 2 c. warm water.

- Most marshmallows are gluten free and egg free, but marshmallow cream contains egg whites.

- Spice packets (example - taco seasoning, etc.) sometimes contain flour to keep the spices from clumping together. Make your own.

- Corn chips and some plain potato chips are gluten free.

- Cool whip is less than 1% dairy.

- Some brands of Worcestershire sauce contain soy sauce that usually contains wheat. Lea and Perrins is gluten free.

- Casein, whey, and lactose are other terms for dairy.

- Some beef consommé, beef broth, and beef bouillon contain wheat. Swanson's is ok.

- Many health food authorities do not recommend using any artificial sweeteners due to possible side effects. I use Stevia which is made from a green leafy plant. I find this product only in Health Food Stores.

- Brown rice syrup and honey can be used in baking.

- Iodized salt contains iodine. Use sea salt instead.

- Canola oil, olive oil, and sunflower oil are recommended.

- Corn tortillas work well for wraps and in Mexican recipes.

Product List

(Our favorite Gluten, Wheat, Dairy, Egg and Peanut Free Products)

If you live in or near a large city these products will be relatively easy to find. Health food stores such as Wild Oats or Whole Foods stock many of these items. Some grocery stores have health food sections and will special order for their customers if you ask. The Stoneridge Orchard dried fruits are available at Sam's and Costco. I have included toll free telephone numbers and web sites for each product when available.

Arrowhead Mills - 800-434-4246 www.arrowheadmills.com
- Wheat Free All Purpose Baking Mix
- Yellow Corn Meal
- White Rice Flour
- Gluten Free Pancake and Baking Mix
- Gluten Free Pizza Crust Mix

Bob's Red Mill Gluten Free - www.bobsredmill.com
- Non-Aluminum Baking Powder
- All Purpose Gluten Free Baking Flour
- Wheat Free Biscuit and Baking Mix

- Tapioca Flour
- Xanthan Gum
- Gluten Free Brownie Mix
- Dairy Free, Gluten Free, Wheat Free, Homemade Wonderful Bread Mix

Chef Williams Cajun Injector - 800-221-8060
- Vegetable Marinade
- Creole Garlic Recipe

I find it at Wal-Mart with the marinades and sauces and at my local grocery store.

DeBoles - rice, lasagna, penne

Droste Cocoa - www.droste.nl

Endangered Species Chocolate Company - www.chocolatebar.com
- Bug Bites - organic dark chocolate squares with bug trading cards

Ener G - 800-331-5222 www.ener-g.com
- Egg Replacers
- Crackers - wheat, gluten, egg, and dairy free
- Tapioca Bread
- Tapioca Hamburger Buns

EnviroKids - www.naturespath.com
- Organic Crispy Rice Bar - (Berry)
- Koala Crisp Cereal
- Vanilla Animal Cookies
- Gorillas Munch Cereal

Food For Life - 800-797-5090 - www.foodforlife.com
- Brown Rice Tortillas (Wheat & Gluten Free)

Frontier Natural Flavors - www.frontiercoop.com
- Simply Organic Flavorings is distributed by Frontier
- Vanilla
- Orange
- Lemon
- Almond

Glutano Gluten Free – 800-363-DIET - www.glutino.com - info@glutino.com
- Apricot Biscuits
- Cream Sandwich Cookies
  - o Zebra Dreams
  - o Vanilla Dreams
  - o Chocolate Dreams

Gluten Free Pantry - 800-291-8386 www.glutenfree.com
- Chocolate Chip Cookie and Cake Mix
- Muffin and Scone Mix
- Perfect Pie Crust
- Chocolate Truffle Brownie Mix
- Angel Food Cake Mix
- Danielle's Chocolate Cake Mix
- Pizza Crust

Kinnikinnick Foods Gluten Free – 877-503-4466 www.kinnikinnick.com
- Crispy Chicken Coating Mix
- Chocolate Cake Mix

Louisiana Cajun Seasoning - 800-356-2905 www.louisianafishfry.com

Nayonaise - 800-848-2769 www.nasoya.com
- Soy based sandwich spread
- Vegi-Dressing

Nonuts Golden Pea butter - www.jsfoods.us

Dr. Oetker Organics - 2229 Drew Rd., Mississauga, Ontario L5S 1E5
- Cooked Pudding & Pie Filling Mix
  (Vanilla, Chocolate, Coconut)

Pamela's Products
- 707-462-6605
- Info@pamelasproducts.com
- Chocolate Cake
- Wheat Free Bread Mix (also use for pizza dough)
- Chocolate Chunk Cookies

Pastas - Rice, Corn, Quinoa (many different brands and types)

Pillsbury Canned Icing – All Flavors

Post Fruity Pebbles

Rapunzel - 800-207-2814 www.rapunzel.com
- Organic Corn Starch

Rumsford - www.clabbergirl.com
- Aluminum Free Baking Powder

San - J Organic Wheat Free Soy Sauce www.san-j.co

Shady Maple Farm ltd – www.shadymaple.com
- Maple Butter
- Maple Sugar (shaker jar)

Simply Organic - distributed by Frontier Natural Products Co-op
Norway, IA 52318
- Dip Mixes - (mix 1 envelope with tofutti sour cream)
  o French Onion
  o Creamy Dill

Spectrum Organic - www.spectrumorganics.com
- All Vegetable Shortening
- Spectrum Canola Spray Oil (high heat)

Stoneridge Orchards - 866-759-5274 - www.stoneridgeorchards.com
(available at Sam's Club and Costco)
- Dried Fruits:
    o Green Apples
    o Raspberries
    o Blueberries
    o Berry Mix

Tinkyada - spirals, lasagna, penne, spinach, spaghetti

Tofutti
- Sour Cream
- Cream Cheese

Tropical Source - www.tropicalsourcecandy.com
- 100% dairy Free Gluten Free Chocolate Chips

Vance's DariFree, Fat Free, Non Dairy Milk Alternative (Potato Milk)
- 800-497-4834 www.vancesfoods.com

Walnut Acres Organic Fruit Squeezes - 800-434-4246 www.
walnutacres.com
- Applesauce in Tubes

Frozen Gluten Free Products

Applegate Farms - distributed by : Groveland Trading Branchburg, NJ 08876 - (no nitrates and no antibiotics added)
- Natural Uncured Beef Hot Dogs
- Natural Uncured Turkey Hot Dogs
- Natural Uncured Chicken Hot Dogs
- Deli Meats (no nitrates or antibiotics added)

Food For Life - 800-797-5090 www.foodforlife.com
- Wheat and Gluten Free Rice Bread
- Wheat and Gluten Free Brown Rice Bread (fruit sweetened - need to heat or toast - good with jam)

Ore Ida Potatoes
- Hash Browns
- Tator-tots
- French Fries

Van's Gluten Free Buckwheat Waffles with Wild Blueberries and Raspberries - www.vanswaffles.com

Wellshire Kids - www.wellshirekids.com
- Chicken Bites (dinosaur shaped breaded bites)

BREADS AND
BREAKFAST FOODS

Basic Recipe for Breakfast Muffins

Ingredients:
- 1 ½ c. Arrowhead Mills Wheat Free All Purpose Baking Mix
- ½ c. Bob's Red Mill Tapioca Flour
- ½ c. Bob's Red Mill Wheat Free Biscuit & Baking Mix
- ½ t. Baking Powder
- 2 Ener-G Egg Replacers
- 2/3 c. sugar
- ½ c. Canola oil
- 1 c. Vance's Powdered Milk (mix one slightly heaping c. to 2 c. warm water)
- 1 t. gluten-free vanilla
- ½ c. applesauce

Directions:
- Mix ingredients (mix by hand)
- Spray muffin tins with Spectrum Canola Oil Spray.
- Add batter to muffin tins
- Bake at 350 degrees for 20-22 minutes

Hints:
- Freezes well.
- Get creative and try some other flavors:
  - Cinnamon
  - Banana (use 3 ripe mashed bananas)
  - Nut Butter (¼ - 1/3 cup)
  - Golden Raisins
  - Dairy Free Chocolate Chips
  - Dried Fruits (Blueberries, Raspberries, Strawberries, Apples)

Our Family Favorite Breakfast Muffin

Make the Basic Muffin Recipe and add:
- 1 t. cinnamon
- ½ c. golden raisins
- ½ c. dried blueberries
- ½ c. Tropical Source Dairy Free, Gluten Free Chocolate Chips
- 3 overly ripe bananas, mashed

Directions:
- Mix ingredients
- Spray muffin tins with Spectrum Canola Oil Spray.
- Add batter to muffin tins
- Bake at 350 degrees for 20-22 minutes

Hints:
- I keep ripe bananas in the freezer. You can thaw at room temperature or in the microwave.
- Keep a mixture of sugar - cinnamon in a small shaker jar. Sprinkle in the bottom of the muffin tins and on top of the batter before baking.
- Do not freeze baked goods containing bananas in the same container with any other baked goods or they will take on the banana flavor.
- When making muffins with banana, reduce Vance's Potato milk to ½ c. to begin. Then if batter is too stiff, gradually add more until the consistency is correct.

Apple Banana Raisin Muffins

Make the basic muffin recipe and add:
- 1 ½ c. dried chopped apples
- 1/3 c. sugar (extra)
- 3 overly ripe bananas, mashed
- ¾ c. golden raisins

Directions:
- Mix ingredients
- Spray muffin tins with Spectrum Canola Oil Spray.
- Add batter to muffin tins
- Bake at 350 degrees for 20-22 minutes

Hints:
- Add an extra ½ c. applesauce if your batter is too stiff.
- Freezes well.

Pumpkin Muffins

Ingredients:
- ½ c. Bob's Red Mill Wheat Free Biscuit and Baking Mix
- 1 ½ c. Arrowhead Mills Wheat Free All Purpose Baking Mix
- ½ c. Bob's Red Mill Tapioca Flour
- 1 c. Sugar
- 1 t. Baking Soda
- ½ t. Baking Powder
- ¾ t. of Sea Salt
- ¾ t. of Cinnamon
- ½ t. of nutmeg
- ½ t. of cloves
- ½ c. canola oil
- ¾ c. Vance's Potato Milk (baking dilution)
- 2 Ener-g egg replacers
- ¾ - 1 can pumpkin

Directions:
- Mix ingredients
- Spray muffin tins with Spectrum Canola Oil Spray.
- Add batter to muffin tins
- Bake at 350 degrees for 20-22 minutes

Hints:
- Try using coconut, chopped nuts or golden raisins
- Try sprinkling the tops of muffins with cinnamon sugar
- You can substitute pumpkin pie spice
  for the nutmeg and cloves.
- Substitute brown sugar instead of white.

Carrot Breakfast Muffins

Make Basic Muffin Recipe and add:
- 1 t. sea salt
- 1 t. cinnamon
- 1 ½ c. shredded carrots
- ¾ c. Golden Raisins
- ¼ c. Vance's Potato Milk (this is in addition to the ½ c in the basic recipe)
- ½ c. Coconut

Directions:
- Mix ingredients
- Spray muffin tins with Spectrum Canola Oil Spray.
- Add batter to muffin tins
- Bake at 350 degrees for 20-22 minutes

Hint:
- Crushed pineapple or cran-raisins is a welcomed addition to the Carrot muffin.
- Try brown sugar instead of white for a little different flavor.

Orange Pineapple Muffins

Make Basic Muffin recipe and add:
- 1 box orange jello (regular or sugar free)
- 1 small can mandarin oranges, drained
- 1 small can crushed pineapple, drained

Directions:
- Mix ingredients
- Spray muffin tins with Spectrum Canola Oil Spray.
- Add batter to muffin tins
- Bake at 350 degrees for 20-22 minutes

Hint
- Save the juice from the canned fruits in case you need to add some of the liquid.
- You can top with lemon or vanilla icing and use these as cupcakes.

Lemon Blueberry Muffins

Make the Basic Muffin recipe and add:
- 1 small box lemon jello. Dry (regular or sugar free)
- 1 -1 ½ c. Blueberries, fresh or frozen (thawed)
- ¼ c. additional Vance's Potato Milk
- 1 t. Frontier Lemon Flavoring

Directions:
- Mix ingredients
- Spray muffin tins with Spectrum Canola Oil Spray.
- Add batter to muffin tins
- Bake at 350 degrees for 20-22 minutes

Hint
- Optional flavors
    o Lemon poppy seed
    o Strawberry
    o Carrot raisin
    o Zucchini

Maple Spice Muffins

Ingredients:
- Gluten Free Pantry Spice Cake & Gingerbread Mix – GF / Wheat Free
- 1 ½ EnerG egg replacer
- 1/3 c. canola oil
- 1 c. Vance's Potato Milk (baking dilution - 1 c. heaping potato milk to 2 c. warm water)
- 2 heaping T. maple butter (Shady Maple Farms – see products page)
- Maple sugar (sprinkle on top)

Directions:
- Mix according to package directions
- Spray muffin tins with Spectrum Canola Oil Spray.
- Add batter to muffin tins
- Sprinkle tops of muffins with maple sugar
- Bake at 350 degrees for 20-22 minutes

Barbara Wells

Breakfast Cookies

Just to come up with a new item that I thought the kids would be excited about, I started experimenting with something that would look like a big cookie but contain the same nutritional ingredients as the breakfast muffins.

The final result is that I use a muffin top pan (which is shallow and much bigger in diameter than a muffin tin. They are a little difficult to find, but try a kitchen store first.

I use the same amount of batter for a breakfast cookie as for a muffin (a very heaping 1/4 cup. Fill it to the top. Bake at 325 for approximately 12-14 minutes. Cool for several minutes on a cooling rack before removing from the pan.

Hint:
- Use an icing tube to decorate the breakfast cookie top with their initial, a flower, etc.

Orange Pancakes

Ingredients:
- Use 1 package Gluten Free Pantry Muffin & Scone Mix

Directions:
- Prepare recipe (back of sack) according to directions using Ener-G egg replacers instead of eggs
- Cook on oiled electric skillet. Do not over cook.
- Serve with pure maple syrup
- If desired, use Fleischman's Unsalted Margarine.

Hint:
- Warm the maple syrup with Fleischman's unsalted margarine and cinnamon for Hot Butter Cinnamon Syrup.
- Pancakes do not freeze well. However, they can be refrigerated (in a zip lock bag) and warmed in the microwave.
- Use pancakes (warmed) for breakfast sandwiches with nut butters and jelly or with breakfast meats.

Biscuits

Ingredients:
- 2 ½ c. Bob's Red Mill Wheat Free Baking and Biscuit Mix
- 1 stick Fleischman's Unsalted Margarine
- Vance's Potato Milk (approx. 1 cup; regular dilution)

Directions:
- Cut together with pastry knife.
- Add Vance's Potato Milk until consistency is right.
- Sprinkle dry mix on the counter or cutting board to roll out dough. I pat out the dough with my hands 1 ¼ to 1 ½ inch thick.
- Cut into biscuits with a glass (approx. 3 inches in diameter)
- Place on a cookie sheet that has been sprayed with Spectra about 2-3 inches apart
- Bake at 375 degrees for about 15-17 minutes until light brown. Do not over bake.
- Makes approximately 12 biscuits

Hint
- Use left over biscuits for mini-sandwiches
- Biscuits warm up well, but they don't freeze well.

Cinnamon Rolls

Ingredients
- 2 ½ c. Bob's Red Mill Baking and Biscuit Mix
- 1 stick Fleischman's Unsalted Margarine
- Glaze:
    - 1 c. powdered sugar
    - ½ t. gluten free vanilla
    - 2 T warm water

Directions:
- Make biscuit recipe.
- Roll dough into rectangular shape. Use the dry baking and biscuit mix to roll dough out on.
- Dot with:
    - Fleischman's Unsalted Butter
    - Brown Sugar
    - Cinnamon
    - 1 T Sugar
- Carefully roll into a long roll. Cut into pieces about 1 ½ inches thick
- Place touching in a prepared pie plate or 9x9 Pyrex.
- Bake at 350 degrees for approximately 25 minutes or until light brown on bottom.
- Mix glaze and spoon over cinnamon rolls while still warm.

Barbara Wells

Danish Rolls

Ingredients:
- 2 ½ c. Bob's Red Mill Baking and Biscuit Mix
- 1 stick Fleischman's Unsalted Margarine
- Vance's Potato Milk – approximately 1 c. (regular dilution)
- Glaze:
  - o   1 c. powdered sugar
  - o   ½ t. gluten free vanilla
  - o   2 T. warm water

Directions:
- Prepare basic biscuit recipe.
- Put the biscuits on the baking pan about 2 inches apart.
- Make an indention on the top of each biscuit with a spoon.
- Put a spoon of jam (I liked the blueberry) into each indention.
- Bake according to biscuit recipe.
- Spoon glaze on top of biscuits as soon as you remove them from the oven.

Strawberry Bread

Ingredients:
- 2 c. Arrowhead Mills Wheat Free All Purpose Baking Mix
- ¾ c. Bob's Red Mill Tapioca Flour
- ¾ Bob's Red Mill Wheat Free Biscuit & Baking Mix
- 1 t. baking soda
- ½ t. sea salt
- 4 Ener-G egg replacers
- 1 ¼ c. oil
- 1 ½ c. sugar
- 1 T. cinnamon
- 1 ½ c. frozen sweetened strawberries, thawed
- ¾ c. English walnuts, chopped

Directions:
- Mix dry ingredients.
- Add remaining ingredients.
- Stir by hand until moistened and mixed well.
- You can bake this either in muffin tins or in mini loaf pans (foil - 5 ¾ x 3 1/3 x 1 7/8)
- Spray the pans well with Spectrum
- Bake at 350 degrees for 22-24 minutes for muffin pans or 50 minutes for the mini loaf pans.

Hint:
- Mash strawberries well before adding to mixture.
- You might want to add coconut or omit the nuts depending upon your preferences
- Freezes well.
- I wrap the loaves in foil.
- Use this batter for Breakfast Cookies

Barbara Wells

Hush Puppies

Ingredients:
- 2 c. yellow gluten free cornmeal (Arrowhead Mills)
- 1 c. Vance's Potato Milk
- 1 t. Sea salt
- 2 t. gluten-free baking powder
- 1 small onion, finely chopped
- 10 dashes red devil cayenne pepper sauce
- Canola oil for frying

Directions:
- Stir dry ingredients together.
- Add liquids.
- Stir well for about 1 minute
- Shape into balls (size of large English walnuts). Balls will be soft.
- Drop into deep fryer pre-heated to 350 degrees. I put oil into a small saucepan on medium heat
- Cook until golden brown on one side. Turn over.
- Best if eaten hot.

Sour Cream Cornbread

This is a cross between spoon bread and corn bread.

Ingredients:
- 1 c. Arrowhead Mills Yellow Cornmeal
- 2 EnerG egg replacers
- 1 - 8 ¾ ounce can cream style corn
- 1 t. Baking Powder
- ½ t. Baking Soda
- 1/2 c. Canola Oil
- 1 1/3 c. Vance's Potato Milk (mix 1 c. slightly heaping powder to 2 c. warm water)
- 1 t. sea salt
- 1 small can chopped green chilies (optional)

Directions:
- Combine all ingredients mixing well.
- Pour into a greased 9-inch square pan.
- Bake at 400 degrees for approximately 30 minutes or until bread is browned.

Hint:
- Refrigerate leftovers.
- Warms up well in microwave.

Cornbread (our favorite!)

Ingredients:
- 1 package Gluten Free Pantry Yankee Corn Bread Mix
- 1 EnerG egg replacer
- 1 1/3 c. Vance's Potato Milk (normal dilution)
- 1 t. lemon juice added to the dairy free milk for the buttermilk substitution
- 1 t. Sea Salt
- 1 T. sugar
- ¼ c. oil

Directions:
- Combine all ingredients mixing well.
- Spray 9-inch square pan with Spectrum Spray
- Pour in mixture and bake at 425 degrees for approximately 25 minutes or until bread is browned.

Hodgson Mill Cornbread

Ingredients:
- Hodgson Mill All Natural Stone Ground Yellow Corn Meal

Directions
- Prepare using recipe for corn meal muffins on back of sack with the following changes:
    - o Use GF flour instead of white flour
    - o Use Vance's Potato Milk
    - o Add 1 t. lemon juice to the potato milk to make the buttermilk substitution.
    - o 1 EnerG egg replacer for the egg
- Bake as directed.

Bob's Red Mill Dairy Free, Gluten Free, Wheat Free Homemade Wonderful Bread Mix

Ingredients:
- Bob's Red Mill D-F G-F W-F Homemade Wonderful Bread Mix

Directions
- Follow directions on back of package for 1 ½ pound bread machine loaf using the following substitutions:
  - o   Use Vance's Potato Milk (regular dilution)
  - o   4 Ener-G egg replacers plus ¼ c. extra water
- Use medium to dark crust setting on your bread machine.
- Bake as directed.

Hints:
- Use for sandwiches or toast
- Fold over a slice to substitute for a hot dog bun
- Slice a little thicker and top with Fleischman's unsalted margarine, garlic, and Italian seasoning. Place under the broiler until browned on top.
- Freezing not recommended.
- Store in refrigerator in plastic bag.

DESSERTS

Angel Food Fruit Cakes

Ingredients:
- 1 package Gluten Free Pantry Angel Food Mix
- 1 can of Wilderness Fruit Pie Filling (Cherry or Blueberry)
- 1 t. gluten-free Vanilla

Directions
- Mix ingredients together by hand until blended.
- Pour batter into a spring form pan. (do not spray pan)
- Bake at 350 degrees until very slightly brown and firm to touch.
- Cool completely.
- Use canned icing to top cake.

Hints:
- Kids love the sprinkles added

Pie Crust

Ingredients:
- 1 package Gluten Free Pantry Perfect Pie Crust

Directions:
- Make according to package directions.

Hint:
- Roll out dough between sheets of wax paper slightly thicker than regular pie crust
- Dough is soft and tears easily, but you can just press it into place.
- Pie dough bakes a pretty golden color and has great taste
- You might need to increase baking time a couple of minutes.

Cherry Cobbler (family favorite)

Ingredients
- 2 cans pie cherries packed in water
- 1 ½ - 1 ¾ c. sugar
- 1 can water
- Pinch of salt
- 1 t. cinnamon
- Red food coloring
- 1 t. gluten-free vanilla
- 1 t. gluten-free almond flavoring
- 2 T Fleischman's unsalted margarine

Directions
- Prepare Gluten Free Pantry Perfect Pie Crust Mix.
- Chill dough.
- Roll out 1/3 of dough between sheets of wax paper.
- Spray 9x13 glass pyrex pan with Spectrum
- Cut dough into strips and place in the pan.
- Combine ingredients listed above in sauce pan and cook until mixture begins to boil.
- Pour mixture over crust strips in pan.
- Roll out second 1/3 of dough. Lay strips on top of the cherries and poke down into the mixture.
- Roll out third 1/3 of dough. Lay strips on top of the cherries.
- Dot the top of the dough with pieces of Fleischman's unsalted margarine and sprinkle with cinnamon and sugar.
- Bake 350 until golden brown. (The dough in the center of the cobbler will be soft and tender.)

Hint:
- Serve warm or at room temperature.
  Warms up well in the microwave.
- Serve plain, with cool whip or vanilla soy ice cream.

Applesauce Chocolate Chip Cake
(family favorite)

Ingredients
- ½ c Spectrum Shortening
- 2 Ener-G egg replacers
- 1 ½ t. Baking Soda
- 1 t. cinnamon
- ½ t. nutmeg
- ½ t. cloves
- 1 ½ c. sugar
- 2 c. Bob's Red Mill All Purpose gluten free baking flour
- 2 T. Droste Cocoa
- 1 - 24 oz. Jar Applesauce

Directions
- Mix shortening and sugar. Add egg replacers.
- Mix dry ingredients together. Add to sugar mixture. Mix well. (I use an electric mixer for this)
- Add applesauce. Mix well.
- Bake in a 9 x 13 Pyrex or in muffin tins, which have been sprayed well with Spectrum spray.
- Sprinkle top with small amount of sugar and tropical source choc chips (dairy free and gluten free)
- Bake at 350 degrees for 20 minutes for cupcakes or 35-37 minutes for cake.
- Test doneness with a toothpick in the center of cake.

Hint:
- Freezes well.

Chocolate Chip Cookies

Start with: 1 package Gluten Free Pantry Chocolate Chip Cookie Mix

Add:
- 1 stick Fleischman's unsalted margarine
- 2 Ener-G egg replacers
- 2 t. gluten free vanilla

Directions
- Partially melt margarine in microwave (approx 45-60 seconds)
- Stir all ingredients together
- Spray cookie sheet with Spectrum or use a silpat mat.
- Place rounded t. of dough (roll in a ball) on cookie sheet and press dough down with fingers to flatten to desired thickness. The dough will not flatten as it bakes.
- Bake 350 approximately 12 minutes. Do not over bake.
- Let cool partially before removing and placing on a cooling rack.
- Store in a plastic container. Freezes well for a short time (2-3 weeks)

Hint:
- Make cookies larger and slightly thicker and bake an extra 1-2 minutes. Put soy vanilla or chocolate ice cream between 2 cookies for ice cream sandwiches.
- Use icing between cookies for sandwich cookie
- If dough is crumbly add 1 T. water to moisten.

Chocolate Cupcakes

Makes about 9 cupcakes.

Start with: 1 package Decadent Chocolate Cake Mix from Gluten Free Pantry

Directions:
- Make according to directions on back.
- Use Ener-g egg replacers for the eggs.
- For the buttermilk, add 1 t. lemon juice to Vance's Potato Milk (mix 1 slightly heaping c. dry milk to 2 c. warm water.)
- Bake in prepared muffin tins or use muffin pan liners to make cupcakes.
- Bake 350 approximately 25 minutes.
- Cool completely and ice as desired.
- Freeze with or without icing.

Hint:
- Using a pastry bag, put vanilla icing inside the cupcakes.
- Frost with flavored icing (chocolate, vanilla or strawberry)
- Top with sprinkles.
- I usually freeze the cupcakes unfrosted and put the icing on as I thaw them.
- If you buy the 5 pound bag, it gives you ingredients based on an 8-inch cake
- Chocolate cake – Bake in a 9x13 pyrex using the directions above

Chocolate Cherry Torte

Directions:
- Prepare Chocolate cake batter. Bake in 2 layers.
- Cool completely
- Beat cream cheese (4 ounces of Tofutti Cream Cheese) with 2 t. lemon juice until smooth.
- Fold in one can creamy vanilla frosting.
- Spread on each layer. Then top with Wilderness Cherry Pie Filling.
- Refrigerate

Hint:
- Use almond flavoring (Frontier brand) in fruit.
- Chill all fillings before combining.

Chocolate Brownie Cake with Chocolate Mocha Icing

Ingredients:
- 1 pkg. Bob Red Mill Gluten Free, Wheat Free, Dairy Free Brownie Mix
- Icing
- 3 T. Droste Cocoa
- 2 T. Fleischman's unsalted margarine, softened
- 3 T. coffee (liquid)
- 2 t. G-F vanilla
- 2 c. Powdered Sugar

Directions:
- Prepare according to pkg. directions. I used Fleischmans Unsalted Margarine,
- 1 Ener-g egg replacer and gluten free vanilla.
- Bake for approximately 25 minutes in a 9x13 Pyrex pan. Do not over-bake. Cool thoroughly before icing.
- Make the icing
- Beat all ingredients with an electric mixer. Adjust powdered sugar if needed to reach desired consistency.

Hint:
- This cake would be great served right away, but it also freezes well.
- Cut the cake into serving pieces and freeze on a cookie sheet. Then, transfer the pieces to a lidded container and separate the layers with sheets of wax paper to avoid sticking.

Ginger Cookies

This was a favorite cookie for my sons their entire lives. This version is almost identical to the original recipe. Kids who love to help with the cooking will enjoy rolling the dough balls in sugar and placing them on the cookie sheet.

Ingredients:
- 1 ½ c. Fleischman's Unsalted Margarine
- 2 c. Sugar
- 2 Ener-G egg replacers
- ½ c. Molasses
- 2 c. Arrowhead Mills Wheat Free All Purpose Baking Mix
- 2 c. Bob's Red Mill Wheat Free Biscuit and Baking Mix
- 1 T. Baking Soda
- 2 t. Ginger
- 1 c. sugar (to roll cookie balls in before baking)

Directions:
- Cream margarine. Add sugar. Cream thoroughly with an electric mixer.
- Add egg replacers and molasses. Beat smooth.
- Add dry ingredients to mixture.
- Mix thoroughly.
- Chill dough until stiff.
- Roll rounded t. of dough into a ball. Roll in sugar.
- Place on a prepared cookie sheet.
- Bake at 350 degrees for approximately 10 minutes.

Hints:
- It's important to let cookies cool on cookie sheet before transferring to a cooling rack.
- Cookies will flatten during cooling.
- Cookies freeze well in tightly closed containers.

Cookie Crust

Ingredients:
- Same as ginger cookies

Directions:
- Flatten cookies with the bottom of a glass dipped in sugar. Bake 12 minutes.
- Freeze. When you need to make a cookie crust, just thaw cookies and make crumbs in a food processor.
- Combine 2 c. cookie crumbs with ¼ c. firmly packed brown sugar, and 5 T. Fleischman's Unsalted margarine (melted and cooled).
- Press firmly into pan.
- Cook 350 10 minutes.
- Let cool before filling.

FAMILY FAVORITES

The following section contains our favorites recipes, which I have been preparing for my family through the years. Many of these recipes needed only minor adjustments to be gluten, wheat, dairy, egg, and peanut free.

Black Bean Mexican Casserole

Ingredients:
- 1 ½ pounds ground beef
- 2 c. chopped onions
- 1 ½ c. green peppers, chopped
- 2 cloves minced garlic
- Taco Seasoning: (This is the equivalent of one envelope of taco seasoning)
  - 2 t. onion powder
  - 1 t. chili powder
  - ½ t. red pepper flakes
  - ¼ t. oregano
  - 1 t. sea salt
  - ½ t. tapioca starch (needed if storing for long period)
  - ½ t. garlic powder
  - ½ t. cumin
- 1 can diced tomatoes
- ¾ c. picante sauce (I use Pace)
- 2 t. cumin
- 2 cans (15 oz) black beans, drained
- 12 corn tortillas (6" size)

Directions:
- Brown meat, onions, peppers, and garlic. Drain.
- Add tomatoes, seasonings, picante, and cumin.
- Boil, then reduce heat and simmer uncovered for 10 minutes.
- Stir in beans.
- Spray 9 x 13 Pyrex pan with Spectrum.
- Spread 1/3 mixture over bottom of pan. Top with 6 tortillas
- Overlap as necessary.
- Add another layer of meat mixture, remaining tortillas, and the last layer of meat mixture.
- Cover with foil and bake at 350 degrees for 30-35 minutes.

Hints:
- If you don't like beans, just omit them.
- If desired, you can serve with the following:
    - Chopped tomato
    - Sliced green onion
    - Sliced ripe olives
    - Sliced jalapenos
    - Tofutti sour cream (dairy free)
- Reheats wells
- I serve Old El Paso Spanish rice as a side. This product is available in most regular grocery stores

Chili

Ingredients:
- 3 - 4 pounds ground chuck or ground round
- 1 large onion, chopped
- 2 cloves garlic, crushed
- 3 - 4 T. chili powder
- ½ T. oregano
- 2 t. sea salt
- 1 T. cumin
- 2 - 1 lb. cans diced tomatoes
- 2 - 1 lb. cans tomato sauce
- Dash red pepper flakes or ground red pepper

Directions:
- Brown meat, onion, and garlic. Drain
- Add remaining ingredients.
- Cover and simmer for 4 hours - longer if you can.

Hints:
- Make ahead (flavor improves with time)
- Serve with Fritos to make Frito Chili Pie
- Kids like to use Doritos Scoops
- Serve with Pasta (rice, corn, or quinoa) for 2 way chili or add kidney or pinto beans for 3 way chili
- Freezes well.

White Chicken Chili

Ingredients:
- 2 pounds cooked chopped chicken
- 5 cans great northern beans (15 ounce size)
- 5 cloves garlic, chopped fine
- 2 yellow onions, chopped
- 1 can chopped green chilies
- 3 c. chicken broth
- 1/3 c. chopped jalapenos
- 1 t. chili powder
- 1 t. cayenne pepper
- 1 T. cumin
- 1 t. red devil cayenne sauce
- 1 T. wheat-free soy sauce
- 1 - 16 oz. diced tomatoes, drained
- 2 t. oregano
- Add sea salt and pepper to taste

Directions:
- Cook chicken and chop into small pieces
- Sauté onions and garlic
- Combine all ingredients.
- Cover and simmer for 2 hours - longer if you can.

Spaghetti Sauce

Ingredients:
- 4 lbs. Ground Chuck
- 4 cans tomato sauce (15 ounce size)
- 4 cans stewed or diced tomatoes (15 ounce size)
- 1 large onion
- 1 large green pepper
- 1 t Oregano
- 2 T Parsley flakes
- 1 T Italian seasoning
- 1 T Minced garlic
- ½ t. Thyme
- 2 t. Red pepper flakes
- 1 ½ t. Sea salt
- ½ t. Pepper
- 1 t. Onion powder

Directions:
- Brown meat and onion. Drain well.
- Add other ingredients. Stir occasionally.
- Simmer. I like to cook this all day.

Hints:
- I start with ¼ - ½ t. on the spices. Taste and adjust as needed.
- Serve over pasta (rice, corn, or quinoa)
- Freezes well.

Chicken Rice Soup

Ingredients:
- Whole chicken
- 1 chopped onion
- 3 carrots, chopped fine
- 2 stalks celery, chopped
- 2 chicken bullion cubes
- 8 quarts water
- 1 t. celery salt
- Parsley flakes
- Salt and pepper to taste
- 1 t. tarragon
- 1 ½ t. Poultry seasoning
- 1 ½ t. minced garlic
- ½ t. thyme
- Rice (approximately 2/3 of a 14 oz. Box of instant rice)

Directions:
- Boil one whole chicken with onions, carrots, celery and 2 chicken bullion cubes in 8 quarts of water.
- De-bone and cube chicken
- Add celery salt, parsley flakes, salt, pepper, tarragon, poultry seasoning, minced garlic, thyme
- Add rice
- Cover pot and cook until rice is tender.

Hints:
- I use fresh parsley
- If the soup is too thick just add more chicken broth. Every time you warm up the soup, you will probably need to dilute it with water or chicken broth.
- Brown rice gives the soup a nutty texture and taste.

Potato Soup

Ingredients:
- 4-5 small potatoes
- 2 T. Fleischman's Unsalted Margarine
- ¼ c. chopped onions
- 1 ½ c. Vance's Potato Milk (regular dilution)
- ¼ c. Bob's Red Mill Potato Flour
- 2-3 drops Cayenne Pepper Sauce
- Onion powder
- Sea salt
- Black pepper
- Parsley flakes

Directions:
- Sauté onions in margarine.
- Peel, cut potatoes into small pieces. Cook in water until tender
- Add potato flour to onions
- Stir to blend
- Add potato milk and stir until thickened
- Add potatoes
- Add spices to taste

Stew

This recipe I developed over the years. It is one of my favorites

Ingredients:
- 2 - 2 ½ lbs. Stew meat, trimmed and cut into small pieces
- 8 slices bacon
- 10 - 12 new potatoes
- 1 - 2 onions, chopped
- 16 ounce package of baby carrots
- 2 cans whole kernel corn or frozen corn
- 2 cans green beans, drained
- 3 cans diced tomatoes
- Frozen okra (don't use the breaded okra)
- Minced garlic to taste
- Red wine to taste
- Chili powder to taste
- Red devil cayenne sauce to taste
- Celery salt to taste
- Cajun seasoning to taste
- Salt and pepper to taste

Directions:
- Brown meat and bacon in small amount of olive oil. Drain.
- Add 1 - 2 quarts of water. Cook about 1 hour.
- Add 3 - 4 cloves of garlic. Add all other ingredients.
- Add more water if needed.
- Simmer until done.

Hints:
- Start with a small amount on the spices. It's much easier to add more if needed.

Barbara Wells

Tallerine (goulash)

Ingredients:
- 2 lbs. Ground Chuck
- 1 can whole corn
- 1 can tomato sauce
- 1 green pepper, chopped
- 1 onion, chopped
- 6 stuffed green olives, sliced
- 1 jar chopped pimento
- 5 oz. Pkg. Macaroni (rice, corn, or quinoa)
- 1 t. sea salt
- ½ t. black pepper
- 1 can Roi-Tel tomatoes
- ½ t. chili powder

Directions:
- Sauté meat, onions, and green pepper. Drain
- Cook macaroni until tender.
- Mix everything together. Put in baking dish.
- Bake at 325 degrees for 45 minutes.

Hints:
- Freezes well.

Chicken Noodle Soup

Ingredients:
- 1 whole chicken
- 4 - 5 chicken bullion cubes
- ½ t Tarragon
- ½ t Celery salt
- ½ t Garlic
- Salt and pepper to taste
- 1 c. Carrots, chopped
- 1 c. Celery, chopped
- Mushrooms (canned or in a jar) (6-8 oz.)
- Noodles (rice, corn, or quinoa) (1 package)

Directions:
- Boil 1 chicken and de-bone.
- Add chicken bullion cubes to broth
- Add tarragon, celery salt, garlic, salt, pepper, carrots, celery, and mushrooms
- Add noodles
- Cook until tender.

Hint:
- Start with approximately ½ t on the spices and add more as needed.
- Add more water if needed

Crunchy Salad

Ingredients:
- Dressing
    - 2 T. vinegar (I use white)
    - ½ c. canola oil
    - ¼ c. sugar
    - 1 t. salt
    - ¼ t. pepper
- 1 head lettuce
- 6 slices bacon - cooked and crumbled
- 1/3 c. sliced almonds, toasted
- 1/3 c. sesame seeds, toasted
- 4-6 green onions, sliced (use the green tops also)

Directions:
- Mix dressing and stir well.
- Chill dressing for a minimum of one hour.
- Mix salad
- Add dressing. <u>Toss and serve immediately.</u>

Hints:
- I make extra dressing especially when using a large head of lettuce.
- Toast seeds and nuts together in a pie plate 325 until slightly browned.
- You can substitute sunflower seeds for sesame seeds .
- Salad is not good left over.

Honey Mustard Baked Chicken

Ingredients:
- ¼ c. Fleischman's unsalted margarine
- ½ c. honey
- ¼ c. prepared mustard
- 1 t. dry mustard
- 1 t. Sea salt
- 1 t. curry powder
- 4 chicken breasts, skinned and boneless

Directions:
- Melt margarine in 9 x 13 pyrex pan.
- Stir in remaining ingredients.
- Roll chicken in mixture.
- Arrange in a single layer in sauce.
- Bake at 375 degrees for 1 hour until chicken is tender and richly glazed. (Baste if you remember.)

Hint:
- When cooking 6 - 8 breasts, double the sauce recipe and bake an Extra 15 minutes.
- Warms up well.

Barbara Wells

Garlic Mashed Potatoes

Ingredients:
- Potatoes (4-5 large)
- 3-4 cloves of fresh garlic
- Fleischman's unsalted margarine
- Sea salt and pepper to taste
- Parsley (small amount)
- Vance's Potato Milk, warmed

Directions:
- Peel potatoes.
- Cover with water and add garlic.
- Boil until tender.
- Drain water.
- Add Fleischman's unsalted margarine, sea salt, and pepper, and parsley.
- Warm milk in the pan you cooked potatoes in and add to mixture.
- Mix to desired consistency.

Hint:
- Use an electric mixer for a smooth creamy mashed potato.
- Make potato salad from leftovers using Nayonaise (soy based sandwich spread).
- Make potato pancakes from leftovers. Serve with any meat and vegetable or salad combo.

Rice Dressing

Serves 8

Ingredients:
- 4 c. chicken broth, divided
- 1 ½ c. uncooked long grain rice
- 1 ½ - 2 c. onion, chopped
- 1 ½ - 2 c. celery, chopped
- ½ c. Fleischman's unsalted margarine
- 2 cans (4 oz) mushrooms, sliced
- 3 T. fresh parsley, minced
- 1 -1 ½ t. poultry seasoning
- ¾ t. sea salt
- ½ t. pepper
- ¼ - ½ t. sage
- ¼ - ½ t. thyme

Directions:
- Bring 3 ½ c. chicken broth and rice to boil.
- Reduce heat, cover, and simmer for 20 minutes.
- Sauté onion and celery in margarine.
- Combine rice, mushrooms, parsley, etc. and remaining 1/2c broth
- Spray a 9 x 13 Pyrex pan with Spectrum spray .
- Bake 350 for approximately 40 minutes or until bubbly.

Hints:
- Warms up well.
- When warming up, add some chicken broth or water for extra moisture.

Barbara Wells

Chicken Salad

Ingredients:
- Chicken breasts or tenders
- Celery salt
- Sweet pickle relish
- Onion powder
- Dried dill weed
- Parsley (fresh or dried)
- Sea salt and pepper
- Nayonaise (soy based sandwich spread)

Directions:
- Cook chicken tenders in water until tender.
- Let chicken cool for 10-20 minutes.
- Chop by hand or in a food processor (pulse so as not too pulverize the chicken)
- Add remaining ingredients

Hint:
- Can also be served on biscuits or homemade bread
- Serve with fruit on the side.

Mexican Vegetable Salad

Ingredients:
- 2 – 15 ounce cans Red kidney beans, drained
- 2 – 12 ounce cans whole kernel corn, drained
- 2 – 3 1/4 oz. ripe olives, sliced
- 1 c. green onions and tops, sliced
- ½ c. green pepper, diced
- 2 T. dried minced onion
- Dressing:
  - 1 c. Nayonaise (soy based sandwich spread)
  - ¼ c. chili sauce
  - 4 t. red wine vinegar
  - 1 t. chili powder
  - Dash of dry mustard
  - Red devil cayenne sauce - to taste
  - ½ t. sugar
  - 2 T. jalapeno peppers, chopped
  - ¼ c. sweet pickle relish

Directions:
- Mix dressing and pour over vegetables.
- Prepare the day before serving.

Summer Squash and Corn

Serves 8

Ingredients:
- ¼ c. onion, chopped
- 2 T. Fleischman's unsalted margarine
- 10 ounce package frozen corn
- 3 medium tomatoes, diced
- 4 medium zucchini, sliced thin
- ½ t. sugar
- ¾ t. oregano
- Salt & pepper to taste

Directions:
- Sauté onion in margarine.
- Add all ingredients.
- Stir until it boils.
- Cover and simmer on low for 20 minutes.

Hints:
- Adjust seasonings if desired.
- Mixture will be thick.
- Serve hot. Warms up well.

Chicken Artichoke Pasta

Serves 4

Ingredients:
- Portabella mushrooms
- Canned artichoke hearts, drained
- Tomato, chopped
- ½ c. blue tick dressing (raspberry salad dressing)
- 1 T. Wheat Free Soy Sauce
- ½ t. hot oil (oriental oil)
- 2 T. balsamic vinegar
- Sliced black olives (optional)
- Parsley
- Chopped walnuts (optional)

Directions:
- Roll chicken tenders in rice flour.
- Sauté until golden brown in olive oil and set aside.
- In same pan combine mushrooms, artichoke hearts and tomatoes
- Cook vegetables partially then add dressing, soy sauce, hot oil and vinegar
- Return chicken to pan. Continue to cook.
- Serve over pasta (rice, corn, or quinoa)
- Sprinkle with sliced black olives, parsley, and chopped walnuts if desired)

Hints:
- I usually consider 3-4 chicken tenders to be one serving.

Corned Beef Brisket with Mustard Glazed Vegetables

Ingredients:
- 2 ½ - 3 ½ pounds Corned beef brisket
- 1 c. water (to cook cabbage and carrots)
- 1 c. julienne carrots
- 8 c. cabbage, sliced about ½ inch thick
- 1 T. Dijon mustard
- 3 T. Fleischman's unsalted margarine
- 1 T. fresh parsley, chopped
- 3 T. red current jelly, melted

Directions:
- Put meat in roast pan. Cover with water.
- Cover Pan and simmer 3 - 3 ½ hours until tender.
- 20 minutes before serving, bring water to a boil in electric skillet.
- Add cabbage and carrots.
- Reduce heat, cover and simmer 15 - 20 minutes until crisp tender.
- Pour off liquid.
- Combine margarine and mustard and add to vegetables.
- Toss lightly to coat.
- Sprinkle with Parsley
- Put brisket fat side up on a rack on broiler pan.
- Brush with melted jelly over the meat and broil 5 minutes until glazed.
- Cut meat across grain.

Brisket

Ingredients:
- 3 oz. Bottle of liquid smoke
- 5 - 6 lbs. Beef brisket
- Celery salt
- Onion salt
- Garlic salt
- Sea salt / pepper
- Lea and Perrins Worcestershire Sauce
- K C Masterpiece Bar-B-Q Sauce

Directions:
- Season meat with the celery, onion, and garlic salts on both sides of brisket.
- Place brisket fat side up in a 9 x 13 Pyrex pan
- Pour ½ bottle of liquid smoke on each side. Cover with foil and marinate in the refrigerator over-night.
- The next day, drain liquid
- Add Salt and pepper and sprinkle with Lea and Perrins Worcestershire sauce.
- Seal tightly in foil. Put in a 9 x 13 pan for baking.
- Bake at 275 degrees for 1 hour for each pound of meat.
- Open foil. Pour bar-b-q sauce over top of brisket. Re-close foil and cook for one more hour.
- Cut meat across the grain.

Hint:
- I use KC Masterpiece because I like the flavor and I know that the Ingredients fit this diet. There are many other brands that you could use. Just check the ingredients on each one.
- If you want, you can skip the bar-b-q sauce completely.
- The pan drippings can be used as a sauce for the meat.
- Warms up and freezes well.

Bean Jalupa

Ingredients:
- 2 lbs. Pork Roast
- ¼ t. Tabasco or Red Devil Cayenne Sauce
- 1 T. Cumin
- 3 c. dry pinto beans
- 2 T. chili powder
- 1 can rotel tomatoes
- 1 t. oregano
- 1 t. sea salt
- 2 cloves garlic
- lg. Onion, chopped

Directions:
- Put all ingredients in crock-pot. Cover with water. Cook all day.
- When meat is tender, tear into pieces and return to pot.
- Serve on Fritos or corn chips.
- Add any of the following:
  - Chopped tomatoes
  - Black olives, chopped
  - Lettuce
  - Onion, chopped
  - Picante sauce

Borracho Beans

Ingredients:
- 1 T. olive oil
- ½ med onion, chopped
- 1 stalk celery, chopped
- ½ green pepper, chopped
- ½ jalapeno, chopped
- 2 cloves garlic, minced
- 1 t. chili powder
- 1 t. cumin
- 1 tomato, chopped
- 1 T. bacon bits
- 1 c. gluten free beer (or water)
- ½ c. fresh cilantro, finely chopped
- Sea salt / pepper to taste
- 2 - 15 oz. cans pinto beans, drained and rinsed

Directions
- Sauté onion, celery, green pepper, jalapeno, and garlic for 5 minutes
- Add all other ingredients (except beans and beer).
- Cook 5 minutes
- Add beans and beer.
- Simmer 20 minutes until sauce is not runny.
- Garnish with cilantro if desired.

Spinach Salad

Serves 4

Ingredients:
- Fresh spinach
- Cooked bacon, crumbled
- Mandarin oranges, drained
- Tomato slices
- Dressing:
  - ¼ c. ketchup
  - ¼ c. sugar
  - ¼ red wine vinegar
  - ¼ c canola oil

Directions:
- Cook bacon, let cool and crumble into small pieces
- Mix spinach, bacon, mandarin oranges and tomatoes
- Mix dressing and stir well

Hint:
- Adjust amount of dressing for the amount of other ingredients.
- You can make individual salads or one large salad

Shoe Peg Corn Salad

Ingredients:
- 1 can French style green beans, drained
- 2 small cans shoe peg corn, drained
- 1 small jar chopped pimento
- 1 diced green pepper
- 1 c. diced celery
- 1 bunch chopped green onions and tops
- ¾ c. vinegar
- 1 T. water
- ½ c. canola oil
- 1 t. sea salt
- 1 c. sugar
- 1 t. black pepper

Directions:
- Bring liquids to a boil.
- Let cool.
- Add salt, sugar & black pepper
- Pour over other ingredients
- Refrigerate over-night before serving

Pork Chops and Rice

Ingredients:
- 8 pork chops
- 1 medium onion, chopped
- 1 c. uncooked rice (converted or instant)
- 1 can chicken broth
- 1 c. water
- 1 T. chicken bullion granules
- ½ t. minced garlic
- Sea salt / pepper to taste

Directions:
- Brown chops slowly, but not too brown
- Sauté onions in grease from chops.
- Mix all ingredients. Put in 9 x 13 Pyrex pan that has been Sprayed with Spectrum
- Lay chops on top. Cover tightly with foil.
- Bake at 300 degrees for 90 minutes

Chicken Wheels

Ingredients:
- Uncooked bacon, cut in half crosswise
- Chicken tenders, trimmed
- Canned whole green chilies, cut into pieces
- Round toothpicks
- 2 zip lock bags

Directions
- ½ piece of bacon, topped with a chicken tender, a piece of green chili.
- Roll up, skewer with a couple of round picks.
- Put wheels in a double zip and lock bags.
- Use a marinade that is gluten, wheat, dairy, egg, and peanut free. (Check the recipes in the marinade section or use wheat free soy sauce)
- Place in the refrigerator. Turn bag occasionally to disperse the marinade.
- Grill approximately 20 - 25 minutes over medium heat or until done.

Hints:
- I make about 6 wheels at a time on a cutting board - assembly style.
- Toothpicks often puncture the bag so I use two and still put the bag in a pan or on a cookie sheet to avoid making a mess
- Soak toothpicks in water to keep them from burning

Cajun Chicken Jambalaya

6 servings

Ingredients:
- Olive oil
- 1 lb. Chicken breasts, skinless and diced
- 2 oz. Bacon, chopped
- ¾ c. onion, chopped
- ¾ c. celery, chopped
- 1 ½ t. minced garlic
- ¾ c. green pepper, chopped
- 1 c. rice, uncooked (instant)
- 1 T. chili powder
- ½ t. - 1 ½ t crushed red pepper (adjust per your heat tolerance)
- ½ t. - 1 t. Cajun seasoning (to taste)
- 2 cans (3c.) tomato sauce
- 1 ½ c. chicken broth
- Parsley
- Sea salt / pepper

Directions:
- Sauté chicken in small amount of olive oil until done. Put aside.
- Sauté bacon with onion, celery, and green pepper for 5 minutes.
- Add rice, chili powder, and red pepper. Cook 5 minutes.
- Add tomato sauce, chicken broth, and spices. Simmer 15 min.
- Add cooked chicken. Simmer 15 minutes.

Hints:
- Warms up well.
- Freezes well.

Vegetables

Vegetables are plentiful and accessible through out the year. You can use fresh, frozen, or canned. They can be prepared many different ways. I cannot think of a single vegetable that would not be acceptable if prepared with proper ingredients.

One or our favorites is Mixed Vegetables using the following:
- Frozen corn
- Frozen mixed vegetables
- Frozen okra (not breaded)
- Chopped onion
- Sea salt /pepper
- Fleischman's unsalted margarine
- Cajun seasoning

Mix all together. Microwave. Stir. Microwave again until done.

Sautéed Zucchini

Sauté sliced zucchini in olive oil with garlic and / or onion.

When almost done, sprinkle with wheat free soy sauce or Balsamic vinegar. (We prefer the vinegar). Season with sea salt and pepper.

Mashed Cauliflower

Ingredients:
- Cauliflower
- 2-3 T Fleischmans Unsalted Margarine
- ½ - 1 t. sea salt
- ½ t. black pepper

Directions:
- Cook 1 head of cauliflower until soft.
- Drain. Use the same pan to warm a small amount of Vance's Potato Milk.
- Using an electric mixer, add margarine and spices
- Add the warm milk slowly until you have the right consistency.

Hint:
- This recipe has been a hit with people who don't necessarily enjoy cauliflower prepared other ways.

MARINADES

Marinade #1

Ingredients:
- 2 c. pineapple juice
- ¾ c. wheat free soy sauce
- Pinch ginger
- 1 T. brown sugar

Directions:
- Boil 5 min. Pour over chicken. Marinate for 4 hours. Grill.

Hint:
- Grill pineapple rings with chicken. Serve over the chicken or separately.

Marinade #2

Ingredients:
- 1/3 c. Hoisin Sauce
- 1/3 c. wheat Free Soy Sauce
- 1/3 c. Sugar
- 1/3 c. Brown Sugar
- 1/3 c. White wine
- Garlic Salt to taste

Directions:
- Marinate chicken or pork over-night.
- Cook in oven or on grill.

Marinade and Basting Sauce #3

Ingredients:
- 1 lb. Fleischman's unsalted margarine
- 1 T. garlic salt
- 3 T. paprika
- 2 T. black pepper
- 1 T. salt
- 1 t. red pepper flakes
- 1 c. wine vinegar

Directions:
- Melt margarine in pan on low heat.
- Add vinegar and remaining ingredients
- Brush sauce on chicken or ribs. Let stand 30 min.
- Stir and baste as you grill meat.

Meat Marinade #4

Ingredients:
- ¼ c. wheat free soy sauce
- 3 t. honey
- 2 T. wine vinegar
- ½ t garlic powder
- ½ t. ginger
- ¾ c. canola oil
- 2 T. onions, chopped

Directions:
- When marinating flank steak, allow 14 - 16 hours.
- Use no longer than 3 days
- Keeps up to 6 weeks
- Use for ka-bobs with sirloin cubes

Barbara Wells

Taco Seasoning Mix

Lots of recipes call for taco seasoning, but you will be safer to make your own from spices that you know are gluten free. Seasoning packets often contain flour to prevent clumping. Check often with manufacturers to keep track of ingredient changes.

(www.gfcfdiet.com)

Ingredients
- 2 t. onion powder
- 1 t. chili powder
- ½ t. crushed dried red pepper
- ¼ t. oregano
- 1 t. sea salt
- ½ t. tapioca starch
- 1 t. garlic powder
- ½ cumin
- ½ t. black pepper

Directions
- Mix all ingredients and store in an airtight container. This makes the equivalent of one envelope of taco seasoning.

  Note: Recipe from Lisa Lewis's Special Diets for Special Kids Volume 2

Season Salt

- 2 T. Sea sat
- 1 t. sugar
- ½ t. paprika
- ¼ t. tumeric
- ¼ t. onion powder
- ¼ t. garlic powder
- ¼ t. potato starch

Directions:
- Combine.
- Store in a small container tightly sealed.

This recipe is from Lisa Lewis's Special Diets for Special Kids Vol. 2

Chef Williams Cajun Injector

Ingredients
- Vegetable Marinade
- Creole Garlic Recipe

Use for chickens, turkey and turkey breasts. It adds wonderful flavor.

LUNCH BOX IDEAS AND KIDS SNACKS

Shop for fun lunch boxes and accessories for your children. Wal-Mart and Target carry lots of choices. For hot foods, you need to prime a large-mouth thermos with boiling water for about 5 minutes, empty out the water, and fill with the hot food. This will keep the food warm for a few hours. Be sure not to use a plastic thermos. The boiling water breaks down the plastic and leeches into the food.

Hot lunch ideas:
- Spaghetti
- Chicken & rice
- Stir fry
- Soups
- Wieners
- Chicken nuggets
- Baked potatoes

Cold lunch ideas:
- Deli sandwich with Energ Tapioca Bread or Glutano Crackers, lunchmeat and all the fixings. The dill dip and French onion dip are both good on sandwiches
- PB&J - with nut butter and jelly or jam
- Deli Meat Roll-ups (use a small amount of dip before you roll up meat)
- Dill or French onion Dip with chips and / or veggies
- Soy yogurt - Fairfield Farms - O Soy
- Soy Pudding C. - O Soy - Zen Soy

Cracker Jacks

Ingredients:
- 2 c. brown sugar, packed
- ½ c. pure maple syrup
- 1 stick Fleischman's unsalted margarine
- Pinch of cream of tarter
- 1 t. baking soda
- 5 quarts popped pop corn (Read the labels carefully and chose one without dairy)
- 3 c. nuts (I use almonds, pecans, and English walnuts)

Directions:
- Boil sugar, syrup, margarine, and cream of tarter for 5 minutes.
- Quickly stir in soda.
- Pour mixture over popcorn and nuts. Mix thoroughly.
- Spread on 2 cookie sheets that have been sprayed with Spectrum.
- Bake at 200 degrees for 40 minutes.   Stir every 10-15 minutes.
- Remove from oven and let cool
- Crumble up for cracker jacks.
- Store in zip lock bags or container.

Hint:
- 5 quarts of popcorn is the equivalent of 2 ½ bags of microwave popped corn.
- Freezes well.
- When cooking the sugar / syrup mixture, stir constantly as mixture tends to boil over.

Trail Mix

Ingredients
- Miniature marshmallows
- DariFree choc chips
- Almonds/ English walnuts / pecans
- Dried fruits
- Raisins
- Sunflower seeds
- Gluten free pretzels
- Enviro kids - gorilla munch cereal
- Rice Chex cereal
- Corn Chex cereal

Directions
- Mix all ingredients together. Store or freeze.

Hot Chocolate

Use the Droste cocoa powder and Vance's potato milk diluted to normal strength with gluten free vanilla. Use the recipe on the Droste box and top with miniature marshmallows.

Dips and Chips

Mix simply organic dip mixes with Tofutti sour cream. Dip with GF chips (Fritos, Plain Lays, etc) or with fresh veggies.

Bug Bites

Organic dark chocolate squares with a bug - trading card.

Use seasonal napkins, fun utensils and seasonal candies (such as tiny candy corns and pumpkins for Halloween and Thanksgiving). This just makes their lunch boxes more fun.

Popsicles - Read labels because some contain dairy.

Nut butters with jelly or jam on gluten-free crackers and breads.

Popcorn - read label closely. Some brands of popcorn contain dairy

    I use Act 11 kettle corn a lot for the kids.

Fruit Chews - many brands are ok

Fresh fruits and vegetables

Snack Mix

Ingredients:
- 1 c. canola oil
- 2 packages of Simply Organic Dip
  Mixes: French onion or dill.
- 1 T. dill weed if you use the dill dip mix or 2 T.
  if you use only the French onion dip mix.
- Approximately 30 ounces of Rice Chex and Corn Chex cereal
- Gluten free pretzels
- Nuts (I use almonds, English walnuts, and pecans.

Directions:
- Mix ingredients well and pour over cereal.
- Store in a large container in the refrigerator.
- Stir several times.
- The next day add gluten free pretzels and nuts.
- Divide into smaller containers .
- Freezes well.

Pizza

Ingredients
- 1 pkg. Gluten Free Pantry Pizza Dough Mix or Pamela's Pizza Crust Mix.
- 1/2 jar spaghetti or pizza sauce
- Pepperoni
- Italian sausage

Directions
- Prepare according to directions on box.
- After dough rises, spread dough on silpat on a cookie sheet or directly on a greased cookie sheet.
- Dough is a little tricky to work with. Use a piece of wax paper to help you pat the dough down to the desired thickness.
- Sprinkle dough with Italian seasoning or oregano.
- Add sauce and toppings
- Bake at 450 degrees 15 - 20 minutes or until edges are brown.

Hint:
- Add oregano to the dough while mixing to add more flavor.
- You can use toppings of your choice. Italian Sausage, Canadian Bacon (it's cut in small circles like pepperoni), pepperoni (regular or turkey) are all flavorful choices.

Tacos

Ingredients:
- 1 ½ lbs. ground turkey, beef, emu, etc.
- 1 small onion
- 1 small can green chilies
- 1 recipe taco seasoning

Directions:
- Sauté meat and onion.
- Add green chilies.
- Add taco seasoning.

Hint:
- Serve with refried or black beans, lettuce, tomatoes, and raw onions
- You can use hard corn taco shells or flat corn tortillas.
- Top with salsa, Tofutti sour cream and guacamole

Guacamole

Ingredients:
- 3 avocados
- 1 t. lime juice
- ½ c. salsa
- 1 - 3 cloves minced garlic
- ½ - ¾ t. onion powder

Directions:
- Peel avocados
- Smash with a fork until desired consistency
- Add remaining ingredients and mix well.
- Add more salsa and limejuice as desired.

Cocktail Wieners

Ingredients:
- 1 package wieners
- ½ c. chili sauce
- ½ c. grape jelly
- 1 ½ T. lemon juice
- 2 ½ t. prepared mustard

Directions:
- Cut wieners into bite sized pieces
- Blend ingredients in pan.
- Stir in wieners.
- Heat until bubbling.
- Simmer about 15 minutes.

Pigs In A Blanket

Ingredients:
- 1 package wieners
- Biscuit dough

Directions:
- Wrap wieners in biscuit dough which has been rolled out about ½" thick.
- Place on a baking pan that has been sprayed with spectrum
- Bake 375 approximately 15 minutes
- Dip in mustard or ketchup

Strawberries with Strawberry Jamaica Dip

Ingredients:
- 1 - 3 ounce package Tofutti Cream Cheese, softened
- ½ c. brown sugar
- 1 ½ c. Tofutti Sour Cream
- 2 T. orange juice
- 1 quart fresh strawberries

Directions:
- Beat cream cheese medium speed till smooth.
- Add sugar, sour cream, and orange juice.
- Mix well.
- Use berries to dip.

Chocolate Dip

Ingredients:
- DariFree chocolate chips
- 1 t. of Spectrum shortening.
- Strawberries, gluten-free pretzels or nuts

Directions:
- Melt chocolate chips
- Add Spectrum shortening.
- Dip the items in the chocolate mixture and place on wax paper on a tray.
- Refrigerate for 60 minutes and enjoy.

Basic Dip

I use simply organic dip mixes.

Ingredients:
- Simply organic dip mix (French Onion or Creamy Dill)
- 1 carton of Tofutti Sour Cream

Directions:
- Mix and enjoy

Hint:
- Good with veggies or corn chips.
- Try on a baked potato for something different

Planning for
Special Occasions

My husband and I are retired and live full-time on a lake in Oklahoma. We have four grandchildren - Dylan and Jordan, ages 7 and 6, who live in Houston; and Brandon and Maria, ages 7 and 5, who live in Kansas City.

We want our grandchildren to have the ultimate lake / family experience on every visit. The four kids get together at our home only once or twice a year, so we have "Camp Grandma and Grandpa" to embrace every opportunity for fun and bonding.

We are building a base of memories with boating, fishing, sea-do and ranger rides, swimming, fire work displays, and slumber parties.

Another fun activity for all of us is the traditional wiener roast. Weather is not a factor. We have them any time of the year. We roast the hot dogs on skewers over the fire pit, keep the chili hot on the charcoal grill, and spread blankets on the ground for eating. The kids love to roll down the grassy hill and we end the evening with a fire works display. What could be more fun?

You must realize that as you build memories with your children and Grandchildren that food is a vital part of the picture. I wanted all of the kids to share in this aspect also. So, now they do. I prepare the same foods for the most part for everyone now, and you can also.

Special occasions, holidays, birthdays, etc. can be very stressful, especially for the family who has special dietary needs. In this next section, you will see how to make those special times simpler and more rewarding. With a little planning and organization, you will be amazed how easy this can be. With all the resources at hand, you and your family should be able to enjoy celebrating every special occasion that comes your way.

HOLIDAY BRUNCH

Menu:
- Macadamia Nut Banana Pancakes
- Sugared Bacon
- Curried Fruit Compote
- Strawberries with Strawberry Jamaica Dip
- Champagne Punch, Mimosas or Bloody Marys (Adults Only)
- Coffee

Macadamia Nut Banana Pancakes

Ingredients:
- 1 pkg. Gluten Free Pantry Scone and Muffin Mix
- Energ Egg Replacer
- ½ c. chopped macadamia nuts
- Bananas
- Hot Buttered Cinnamon Maple Syrup

Directions:
- Make orange pancake recipe (bottom recipe on back of sack)
- Substitute Energ Egg Replacer for the egg.
- Add ½ c. chopped macadamia nuts to batter
- After cooking pancakes, add banana
  slices and more chopped nuts.
- Pour hot buttered cinnamon maple syrup over the pancakes.

Hot Buttered Cinnamon Maple Syrup

Directions:
- Add Fleischman's unsalted margarine and cinnamon to pure maple syrup
- Heat until warm.
- Refrigerate left over syrup.

Sugared Bacon

Ingredients:
- 1 lb. Bacon - room temperature (use regular sliced, not thick)
- 1 ¾ c. brown sugar
- 1 T. cinnamon

Directions:
- Cut each slice of bacon in half crosswise.
- Mix sugar and cinnamon
- Thoroughly coat each slice of bacon.
- Place on a rack on a cookie sheet
- Bake at 350 degrees until bacon is crisp and sugar is bubbly. Usually about 15 - 20 minutes. Watch closely as it can burn easily.
- Cool on foil.
- Serve at room temperature. You can make this the day ahead and refrigerate.

Champagne Punch

Ingredients:
- 1/3 c. frozen orange juice concentrate, thawed and undiluted
- ¼ c. frozen lemonade concentrate, thawed and undiluted
- 750 milliliter bottle dry, white wine, chilled
- 750 milliliter bottle champagne, chilled

Directions:
- Stir together.
- Serve immediately over ice.
- This makes six, 2/3 c. servings.

Mimosas

- ½ diluted frozen orange juice
- ½ c. chilled champagne

Make any amount you wish to these proportions.

Bloody Mary's

1 ½ oz. Potato Vodka
1 T lea and Perrins Worcestershire Sauce
½ t. horseradish
Squeeze of lime
½ t. celery salt

Stir the above ingredients together.

Add the following:
V-8 juice or tomato juice
Ice
Stalk of celery or green olive

Hint:
You can salt the rims of the glasses if desired.

Curried Fruit Compote

1 can (20 oz) chunk pineapple
1 can (16 oz) pear halves, cut in 2 -3 pieces
1 can (16 oz) peach or apricot halves, cut into 2 - 3 pieces
Maraschino cherries
¼ c. Fleischman's unsalted margarine
½ c. brown sugar, packed
1 T. cinnamon
Drain fruits, Put into a 1 ½ quart baking dish. Set aside.
Microwave margarine on high 45 seconds or until melted.

Stir in brown sugar and cinnamon. Pour over fruit. Microwave on medium, uncovered 8 - 10 minutes or until heated Through. Rotate dish once or twice. Serve warm.

Strawberries Jamaica

- 1 - 3 oz. package Tofutti Cream Cheese, softened
- ½ c. brown sugar
- 1 ½ c. Tofutti sour cream
- 2 T. orange juice
- 1 quart fresh strawberries

Beat cream cheese medium speed until smooth. Add sugar, sour cream, and orange juice. Mix. Use as a dip for berries.

THANKSGIVING

I hope that your family will thoroughly enjoy this traditional Thanksgiving Feast!

Menu:
- Turkey
- Dressing
- Giblet Gravy
- Garlic Mashed Potatoes (recipe is in the Family Favorites Section)
- Sweet Potatoes with apples, nuts, raisins, and marshmallows
- Strawberry Pretzel Salad
- Cranberry Jello Salad
- Marinated Green Beans
- Biscuits - the biscuit recipe is in the bread and breakfast foods section (Bread & Breakfast Foods Section).
- Desserts - pick any of the desserts listed in the dessert section.

Turkey

Directions:
- Select a fresh or frozen bird that has not been basted with butter, etc.
- Inject marinade into the turkey or turkey breast. I typically use Chef Williams Cajun Injector Marinade. You can find it at Wal-Mart or most local grocery stores.
- It adds a lot of flavor and moistness.
- Bake or smoke the turkey
- Bake at 325 degrees according to the directions or smoke at 225 degrees until fully cooked.

Hints:
- I usually do 2 or 3 turkey breasts instead of a full turkey. It is less mess and less waste.

Dressing

This recipe will feed about 7 - 8 people.

Ingredients:
- 1 pan gluten free corn bread (bread section)
- ½ recipe biscuits (Bread & Breakfast Section)
- 1 c. celery, chopped
- 1 c. yellow onion plus green onions and tops, chopped
- Fresh parsley
- ½ t. sea salt
- ¼ t. cayenne pepper (per taste)
- ¼ t. black pepper
- 2 EnerG Egg Replacers (optional)
- ¼ t. celery salt

- ¾ t. poultry seasoning
- ¼ t. thyme
- ¼ - ½ t. sage
- 1 c giblet gravy
- 1 c. Vance's potato milk, warmed (dilute as you would for baking – 1 heaping cup powder per 2 cups warm water)
- 1 ½ c. chicken broth
- ½ stick Fleischman's Unsalted Margarine

Directions:
- Crumble and dry corn bread and about ½ pan of biscuits. I use more corn bread than bread (about double)
- Crumble the breads and dry out for a couple of days
- Sauté onions and celery in margarine.
- Add warm milk
- Add to breads
- Add all spices
- Add liquids gradually - mixture should not be dry but fairly soupy.
- Spray a 9 x 13 or a 7 x 11 pan with Spectrum.
- Bake at 350 degrees for approximately 1 hour or until browned.

Giblet Gravy

This recipe is based on one quart of chicken broth. You can either boil chickens or use a prepared both such as Swansons 98% fat free chicken broth. This will serve approximately 6-8 people.

Ingredients:
- Swanson's chicken broth - 1 quart
- ¼ t. Sea salt
- ¼ t. Black pepper
- ¼ t. Onion powder
- 1 t. Parsley (fresh if you have it)
- 6 T. GF flour or conrstartch. I use Bob's Red Mill All Purpose Gluten Free Baking Flour.

Directions
- Heat the chicken broth until warm but not boiling.
- Season with sea salt and pepper, and onion powder.
- Thicken with a gluten free, wheat free flour or cornstarch. I like bob's Red Mill All Purpose GF Baking Flour. Mix 6 T. flour with some of the warm liquid and pour through a strainer to avoid lumps. (You will need to do this several times, so it is easier if you add 2 T. of flour at a time)
- After the gravy has thickened, taste and add the seasonings. Adjust as needed. I use more parsley when using fresh.

Hints:
- If you have time, make your own broth for a little better flavor
- If you boil the livers from the chickens and want to add them to your gravy, just chop them fine.
- If the gravy is too thick just dilute with more chicken broth.
- If you make the gravy the day before serving, you might need to add a little more broth when warming it up.

Marinated Green Beans

Ingredients:
- 2 regular size cans cut green beans
- 1 thinly sliced onion
- Sea salt / pepper to taste
- 1 T. canola oil
- 1 T. vinegar
- Sour Cream Sauce
- 1 c. Tofutti sour cream
- 1 t. lemon juice
- ½ - 1 T. horseradish
- 2 t. chopped chives
- ½ c. Nayonaise (soy based sandwich spread)
- ¼ t. dry mustard
- Grated onion, to taste

Directions:
- Mix beans, onion, salt & pepper, canola oil and vinegar
- Let marinate for several hours in refrigerator stirring occasionally
- Drain
- Add sour cream sauce.
  - Combine all ingredients.
  - Mix well and pour over bean salad.

Sweet Potatoes with apples, marshmallows, raisins, and nuts

Ingredients:
- 2 granny smith apples, sliced
- 2/3 c. chopped pecans
- 2/3 c. brown sugar, packed
- 1 t. cinnamon
- 2 - 17 oz. cans sweet potatoes, drained
- ¼ - ½ stick Fleischman's unsalted margarine
- 1/3 - ½ c. orange juice
- ½ c. golden raisins
- Miniature marshmallows

Directions:
- Toss apples, nuts, and raisins with brown sugar and cinnamon.
- Alternate layers with sweet potatoes and apples in 1 ½ quart baking dish (spray with Spectrum)
- Pour orange juice over top and dot with margarine.
- Bake at 350 degrees for 35 - 40 min.
- Place marshmallows on top and broil until lightly browned.
- Watch closely to avoid burning the marshmallows

Strawberry Salad with Pretzel Crust

Ingredients:
- Pretzel Crust
    - 2 c. Gluten Free pretzels, crushed
    - 4 T. sugar
    - ¾ c. melted Fleischman's unsalted margarine
- Cream cheese mixture
    - 8 oz. Tofutti Cream Cheese
    - 8 oz. Cool Whip
    - ¾ c. sugar
- Strawberry Jello
    - 6 oz. Pkg. Strawberry jello (regular or sugar free)
    - 2 c. boiling water
    - 2 - 10 ounce packages frozen strawberries in sugar

Directions:
- Make pretzel crust
    - Mix pretzels, sugar and margarine.
    - Spread in 9 x 13 Pyrex (spray with Spectrum)
    - Bake at 400 degrees for 8 minutes.
    - Cool completely.
- Make cream cheese mixture
    - Mix cream cheese, cool whip and sugar together using electric mixer.
    - Spread over crust and refrigerate.
- Make jello
    - Dissolve jello in water.
    - Add slightly thawed berries.
    - Chill until jello begins to congeal.
    - Stir and spread over cream cheese layer and refrigerate.

Hints:
- Make a day ahead.
- Experiment with different berries and flavors of jello

Cranberry Jello Salad

Ingredients:
- 1 pkg. Cherry jello (large)
- 1 c. boiling water
- 1 can cranberry sauce
- ½ c. Tofutti Sour Cream
- ½ c. pecans, chopped

Directions:
- Mix all ingredients together the day before you plan to serve.

4ᴛʜ ᴏꜰ Jᴜʟʏ Pɪᴄɴɪᴄ ᴏʀ
Aɴʏ Dᴀʏ Wᴇɪɴᴇʀ Rᴏᴀꜱᴛ

Menu
- Hamburgers
- Hot Dogs
- Baked Beans
- Chili (p. 47)
- Corn on the Cob
- Corn Chips with Dip (Lunch Box
  Ideas & Kids Snacks Section)
- Fresh Fruit
- Cookies or Cupcakes
- Lemonade

Hint:
- I sometimes use a slice of the homemade
  bread for a hotdog bun.
- Kinnikuk makes a gluten-free hot dog bun,
  but it does contain egg whites.
- Ener-G makes gluten-free hamburger and hotdog buns.

Barbara Wells

HALLOWEEN HEALTHY TREATS

Ghoulish Hand Treats

Ingredients:
- One box uncoated plastic rubber gloves
- 1 bag of candy corn
- Plain slightly salted GF popcorn
- Orange and black yarn
- Spooky spider rings

Directions
- Put one candy corn in the fingertips of each glove.
- Fill the glove with popcorn.
- Tie off the glove with the yarn.
- Place a spider ring on one finger of each glove

Worm Jello

Ingredients:
- Green jello
- Bag of gummy worms
- Halloween cups

Directions
- Prepare jello in cups.
- Put in refrigerator until almost set
- Add the gummy worms

Pumpkin Faces

Ingredients:
- Rice cakes (mini or large)
- Tofutti cream cheese
- Orange food coloring
- Raisins

Directions
- Mix orange food coloring in cream cheese and spread on rice cake.
- Use the raisins to make the pumpkin face

Barbara Wells

Bug Juice

10 servings

Ingredients:
- 2 – 10 oz. pkg. frozen strawberries, defrosted
- 1 – 6 ox. can lemonade concentrate, thawed
- 1 QT ginger ale
- 2 c. raisins
- 6 gummy bears

Directions
- Mix the strawberries and lemonade concentrate in a blender until smooth and thick
- Gradually add ginger ale
- Transfer the beverage to a punch bowl
- Stir in any remaining ginger ale and raisins
- Place gummy worms on the rim of the bowl

BIRTHDAY CAKES

Sheep Cake

Ingredients:
- Use Danielle's GF Chocolate Cake (Gluten Free Pantry)
- 1 – 9 inch round cake
- 1 small pyrex round bowl (for face)
- 3 cupcakes
- 2 - 3 c. Pillsbury White Icing
- 1 – 2 c. Pillsbury Chocolate Icing
- 3 ½ - 4c. mini marshmallows
- 2 gumdrops or jellybeans (eyes) or Black Icing in a Tube.
- Red shoestring licorice (mouth) or Red Icing in a Tube.

Directions
- Prepare cake mix according to directions in the desert sections
- Place the dome shaped cake upside down in the center of a round cake and secure with icing
- Cut one cupcake in half and use for the ears and use the other two cupcakes for legs. Secure with icing
- Frost the body, the outsides of the ears, and the top halves of the hooves with the white icing.
- Cover with mini marshmallows
- Frost the remaining areas with chocolate icing, then cover with dairy free chocolate chips
- Add eyes, nose and mouth

Hint:
- The applesauce cake also works well with this recipe.

Cow Cake

Ingredients:
- Use Danielle's GF Chocolate Cake (Gluten Free Pantry)
- 1 – 9 inch round cake
- 1 small pyrex round bowl (for face)
- 3 cupcakes
- 2 - 3 c. Pillsbury White Icing
- 1 – 2 c. Pillsbury Chocolate Icing
- 3 ½ - 4c. mini marshmallows
- 2 gumdrops or jellybeans (eyes)
- Red shoestring licorice (mouth) or Red Icing in a Tube.

Directions
- Decorate according to picture

Barbara Wells

Horse Cake

Follow the directions for the other cakes and decorate according to picture.

Hint: Little girls love pink cakes!

Printed in the United States
88035LV00014B/256-276/A